A PUPPY
FOR YOU

A PUPPY FOR YOU

LILO HESS

CHARLES SCRIBNER'S SONS · NEW YORK

My kindest thanks are hereby extended to Mrs. Constance Hubbard of Astolat Sheltie Kennel, Kunkletown, Pa., for her invaluable assistance and for introducing me to the delightful Shetland Sheepdogs.

Thanks also to the breeders and private dog owners who let me photograph their lovely dogs.

Specially: Skippy Kennels, E. Stroudsburg, Pa.: Toy Fox Terriers.

Mayfair Yorkie House, Newton, N.J.: Yorkshire Terriers.

Meadowbrook Kennels, Slingerlands, N.Y.: Welsh Terriers.

Poco Kennels, E. Stroudsburg, Pa.: Great Pyrenees.

Paw Paw Kennels, Floral Park, L.I.: Bichon Frise.

Holidane Kennel, Mt. Bethel, Pa.: Great Danes.

Indian Mt. Kennels, E. Stroudsburg, Pa.: St. Bernards.

Library of Congress Cataloging in Publication Data

Hess, Lilo.
  A puppy for you.

  SUMMARY: Discusses the selection, care, and training of a puppy.
  1. Puppies—Juvenile literature. [1. Dogs] I. Title.
SF426.5.H47   636.7'07   76-17842
ISBN 0-684-14753-X

SHETLAND SHEEPDOG (SHELTIE)

When you have decided to bring a puppy into your family, to be your companion and friend, you must make sure that *you* pick the puppy, and that the puppy does not pick you. Don't be a pushover when you see a puppy in a pet store, at a friend's house, or in a kennel wagging its tail and looking at you with eyes that seem to say: "I am the one for you." It is very hard to resist such "pleading," but this is exactly what you should do, or you might regret your hasty decision later on.

Bringing a dog into your home is something the entire family should carefully think about, not just the one member who will be the actual owner. Before you rush out and get a dog, give some thought to what kind of dog you really like and what kind would fit in well with your way of life.

There are 122 different breeds of dog recognized by the AKC—the American Kennel Club—and several that are not yet recognized. The AKC is the official agency that handles all registrations of purebred dogs in the United States.

Each variety of dog has been selectively bred to perfect its in-born behavior pattern, such as hunting, guarding, herding, re-trieving, tracking, or just being a pet. Some have been bred for their unusual appearance, as small lap dogs or gentle giants. There is a breed of dog to suit everyone's taste.

If your family lives in a small apartment or is on a tight budget, don't get a St. Bernard, an Irish Wolfhound, or a Great Pyrenees no matter how lovable and cuddly the puppies are. If there are very young children in the family, don't get a delicate toy breed. If you like to go for long hikes and roam in the woods or fields, get a sturdy, active breed. If you are a home-body, you will be happier with a quiet dog.

Look at as many different breeds as you can before you make your decision. Get information about their temperament, size, and usefulness. There are many books available that describe all the various breeds. Humane societies, 4-H projects, kennels, and breeders can also give you a lot of information. You can

ST. BERNARD

TOY FOX TERRIER

ENGLISH SPRINGER SPANIEL

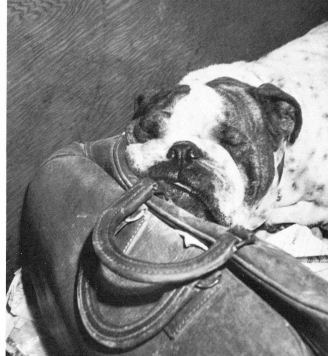

BULLDOG

write to the AKC at 51 Madison Avenue, New York, NY 10010 for the address of a kennel in your neighborhood that handles the kind of dog you are interested in.

At dog shows—which have become so popular that most communities have at least one or two each year—you can see many beautiful dogs and puppies, and their owners are usually happy to tell you about their favorite breed. You must try to get the best kind of dog you can—that is, the best in health and temperament.

ENGLISH SPRINGER SPANIEL, POODLE, BEAGLE, WEST HIGHLAND WHITE TERRIER, SHIH TZU, LHASA APSO, COCKER SPANIEL, DALMATION

A dog's temperament is its emotional behavior. This is hereditary, which means it is passed on from one generation to the next. A dog with a good temperament is usually reliable, affectionate, even-tempered, loyal, and protective without being aggressive. A dog with a bad temperament is usually excitable, jealous, short-tempered, aggressive, and unpredictable.

One of the advantages of getting a purebred dog from a reliable dealer is that you will know exactly what your dog will look like when fully grown and what its temperament and size are likely to be. In a puppy, most of the character traits of the adult dog are not yet developed. All puppies are friendly, lovable, and playful. Many breeds resemble each other in puppyhood, and only someone familiar with the various breeds can tell you the difference.

BICHON FRISE

BEAGLE

YORKSHIRE TERRIER

PUG

GERMAN SHEPHERD

ST. BERNARD

GREAT PYRENEES

AFGHAN HOUND

YORKSHIRE TERRIER   WELSH TERRIER

The two puppies pictured here look very similar to most
people, yet one will grow up to be a Yorkshire Terrier, a silky,

11

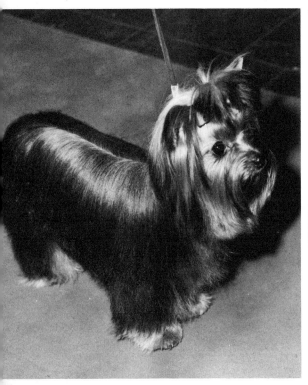

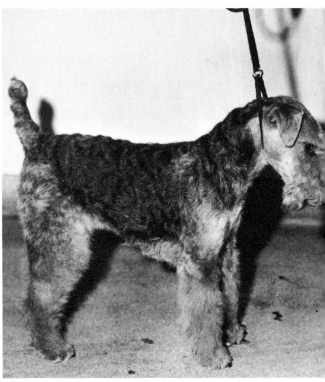

YORKSHIRE TERRIER   WELSH TERRIER

long-haired toy terrier which seldom weighs more than seven
pounds, and which, although it is a charming house pet, is not
suited as a pet for young children. The other is a Welsh Terrier
and will grow up to be a bouncy, playful, and courageous me-
dium-sized dog, an ideal companion for children of all ages. So
if you are shopping for a purebred dog at a kennel, ask to see the
parents of the puppy you choose. Good breeders will be proud
to show them to you.

Not all registered puppies will grow into show dogs. The fact that a pup is registered means only that the pup's mother (dam) and father (sire) are registered. Even a breeder cannot be absolutely sure if a young dog will grow up perfect enough to be entered in a show. The price of a puppy that has show prospects will be much higher than the price of its litter mates. You can often get a well-bred puppy at a reasonable price, just because its tail is an inch too long or too short, or its fur curls the wrong way, or its ears stand erect when they should hang. All these "faults" are of no importance to the pet owner who doesn't plan to show his or her dog.

A purebred puppy is not automatically a good, healthy dog. Some breeders breed inferior dogs just to have a lot of puppies to sell. Be sure you check the reputation of a kennel with a friend, a local dog-fancier group, or the AKC.

If you buy a puppy from a pet shop or a kennel that handles many different breeds, make sure that all the puppies are kept clean, and that their cages are roomy and well ventilated. The

COCKER SPANIEL

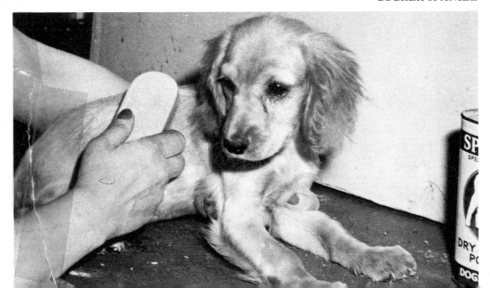

puppies should be active, bright-eyed, and well groomed and fed. If any of them have runny noses, are listless, or live in cramped, dirty cages, not only might they have physical handicaps, but their unhappy surroundings may have influenced their personalities at an impressionable age. Walk away from such a place, no matter how hard it is, and even if the puppy you are interested in seems healthy. If people refuse to buy from badly run pet shops and kennels, the dealers will have to either go out of business or give their animals better care. Regardless of where you buy your puppy, have a veterinarian check it before you pay for it.

If you do not intend to enter shows or obedience exhibitions, if you don't care what pedigree your dog has, and if you don't plan to breed your dog, you should consider giving a home to an abandoned puppy. Your local humane society or animal shelter has many purebred or mixed-breed (mongrel) puppies and dogs just waiting for a loving master. Those organizations will make sure the animal you select is healthy. They can also tell you the breed and approximate age of a puppy, and whether it will remain small or grow to be very large. You can often tell how big a puppy will become by the size and structure of its paws. If they are small and dainty, the dog will probably not be very big, but if the feet are heavy-boned and look like the paws of a teddy bear, be prepared for a large pet.

It is not true that mongrels are smarter, healthier, and more loyal than purebred dogs. Nor is the opposite true. Either kind

MONGRELS

can be of good, sound quality—or high-strung and sickly, with an unsatisfactory disposition. Mongrels often have inferior litters because of unsupervised breeding and poor care. But the healthy mongrel and the healthy purebred dog make equally good, faithful, and lovable pets. Both should be given the same thoughtful attention and care.

The age of the puppy when you get it is very important. If the puppy is only four to six weeks old when it is offered for sale, do not buy it. It is much too young to be on its own. No reliable dealer will sell such a tiny creature.

SHETLAND SHEEPDOGS AT FIVE WEEKS

SHETLAND SHEEPDOG AT SIX MONTHS

On the other hand, a puppy that is four months to one year old has most of its character already formed. It is often attached to its owner and might never fully accept you as its new master. This is particularly so in breeds that are oriented to one master or one family, such as the German Shepherd, the Mastiff, the Doberman, the Collie, and many others.

Only if you are interested in a show dog should you buy an older puppy whose good and bad points are more developed and noticeable. Also, if the dog is to be used for guard duty, as a seeing-eye dog, or for field or obedience work, the older puppy is ready to start its special training. The price for such a dog might be higher than for a younger one. Some breeders like to keep their puppies for a while to be sure they don't sell good show dogs at low pet prices.

A puppy between the ages of eight weeks and fourteen weeks is physically and mentally ready to start a new life. It can eat and digest its food properly, its coordination is good, and it is eager to learn, play, and become totally devoted to its new owner and a happy new member of a human family.

When a puppy is ready to be sold, it probably has had its first shots and may have been wormed. Be sure the seller gives you a health certificate that you can show to your veterinarian, who will then know what additional inoculations your puppy needs and when they should be given.

The question of whether to get a male or a female should also be decided before you buy your dog. Both sexes make equally devoted pets. A female is often more quiet and does not tend to roam as much as a male, but that is not always so. If you have to walk your dog, it might be important to you that a female usually relieves herself more quickly and less often than a male, who likes to sniff about and lift his leg many times. Males are sometimes more aggressive and usually larger than females. A

SHETLAND SHEEPDOGS AT EIGHT WEEKS

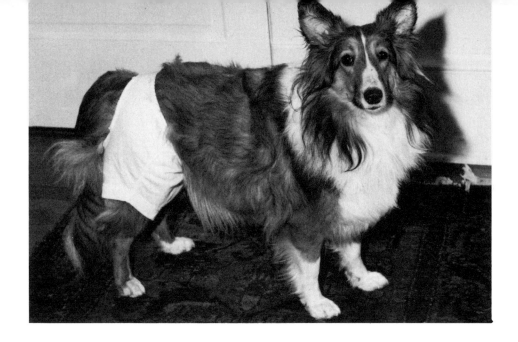

male's fur might be more luxurious than a female's. A female comes into "season" or into "heat" twice a year. This is the time she can mate and become a mother. Since the colored discharge of the dog in season can stain rugs and floors, you might outfit her with a pair of doggie britches, which are sold in pet stores, or a pair of cotton baby panties with a hole cut in them for the tail. A female in season must be guarded closely and kept on a leash at all times. Male dogs can smell a female in heat for miles and will do almost anything to get to her. They might break their leash, jump fences, or swim across a stream.

If you do not intend to breed your dog, it can be surgically fixed so you will not have to worry about runaway dogs or unwanted puppies. Females are spayed; males are altered. It does not change a dog's looks, personality, or usefulness to have this operation. Check with your veterinarian about the best age to have it done.

It is also important to plan the arrival of your puppy in its new home in advance. Don't bring a small puppy home for Christmas no matter how eager you are to have it. The excitement of holiday preparations, friends visiting, noise, and general confusion can frighten and upset the puppy. Ask that the dog be given to you either several weeks in advance or after the holidays are over. All kennels and pet stores will hold a puppy till after the holidays. Your puppy will need a quiet place to come home to, and it should have your undivided attention.

If you spend the summer away from home, do not get a puppy shortly before you leave. You cannot take a young untrained dog with you and you should not board it at a kennel before it has had a chance to get to know you and get established in its new home. Wait till you return from vacation.

If you buy a registered puppy, be sure you get all the papers you need to register it:

1. A bill of sale with the description of the dog.
2. A certificate of transfer of ownership if the puppy has already been individually registered. This must be filled out and the seller must sign it. Then you send it to the AKC so that you can be recorded as the new owner.
3. A registration application form if the puppy has not yet been individually registered (but the litter must have been registered). The seller must sign this. You fill in your puppy's name and return the form with a small fee (printed on the form) to the AKC. A validated certificate will be returned to you.
4. A pedigree certificate (a record of your dog's ancestors).

Keep all the papers in a safe place, because you will need them if you want to enter a dog show, breed your dog, or sell it.

The moment you take possession of your new puppy is an exciting one for both of you. You are now entrusted with caring for a creature with sensitive feelings and special needs.

If your puppy is shipped to you by air freight, be sure to pick it up promptly. The dealer will advise you in advance where and when your puppy is due to arrive.

If you pick the puppy up yourself, it is best to put it in a box or carrier lined with shredded newspaper.

When you arrive home, the puppy will be tired and frightened and confused. Be patient, gentle, and quiet with it. Don't let the entire family or neighbors pet it and fuss over it.

Let it come out of the box by itself when it is ready. You can put the box on its side if the puppy is too tiny to jump out. The

box has become a temporary refuge and the puppy might want to stay in it for a little while and look about. When it comes out, let it rest, explore, or even hide under the furniture. Before long it will come to you.

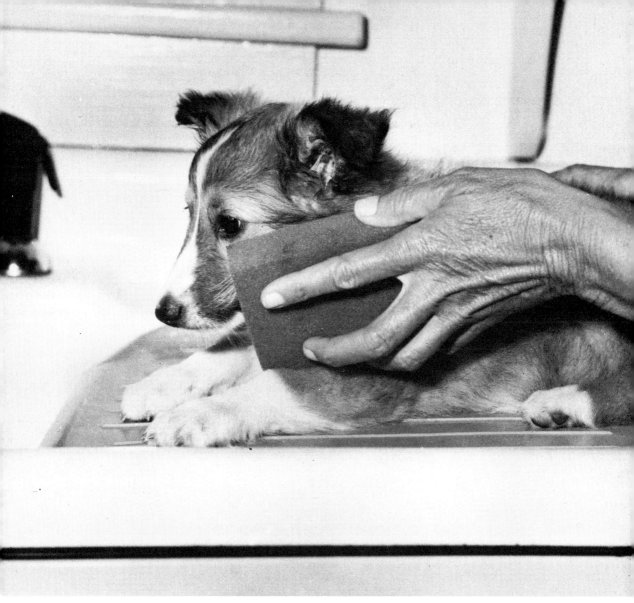

If the puppy has soiled itself or has been car-sick on the trip, do not bathe it, but sponge it off gently with lukewarm water and dry it with a towel.

Start your puppy out with a quiet, sensible routine. The pattern you set at the beginning will be its guideline to future behavior.

Always call your puppy by its name. It will quickly learn to respond to it. Put a lightweight collar on, and make sure it is only tight enough to keep the head from slipping through. Since a puppy grows quickly, check the collar often and readjust it.

Never pick a puppy up by the ears, the front legs, or the scruff of the neck. Put one hand under its chest between the forelegs and support the rear end with your other hand. When you put it down, don't just dump it—make sure all four feet touch the floor.

The place your puppy sleeps the first few nights will be the one it will consider as its own permanent quarters. You can give it a dog bed, a blanket, or a cardboard box in a warm, quiet, out-of-the-way corner. Your pet may prefer to select its own sleeping place. If the place it chooses is convenient for the entire family and the puppy is in no one's way, let it stay there. Should it select a staircase or other unsuitable place, discourage it from the start with a firm *no* and by picking it up and placing it where it should be. You might have to repeat this several times. Sometimes it is advisable to confine a puppy to a certain place or room to keep it out of trouble and out of people's way. Fence off a corner of a room with a gate, boards, or cardboard. Line it with newspaper and put the puppy's sleeping box or blanket inside.

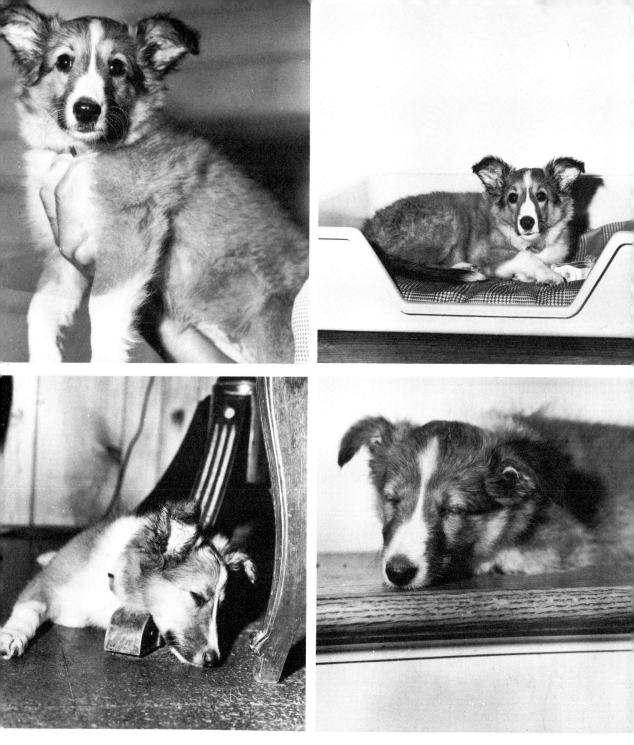

Almost every puppy will cry and yap the first night because it is lonesome and scared. Be patient with it. You might put a hot-water bag filled with warm (not hot) water, or an old ticking alarm clock wrapped in a towel, in its bed. This might soothe it. If you weaken and take it to bed with you, your puppy will be so content that it will demand to keep this comfortable sleeping place from then on. Think twice before you indulge your puppy this way, especially if you have a St. Bernard or a German Shepherd.

Feeding your puppy properly is very important. Since every dog owner and every book will give you different advice, ask the breeder or former owner what the puppy was fed and how often. Stick to this diet until your dog is well adjusted. Then you can gradually change to a food and time that you prefer. If you have no diet and do not know what to feed your dog, or which food is best, check with your veterinarian. The younger the puppy is, the more often it should eat. A pup two months to six months old should be fed four times a day: morning, noon, afternoon, and evening. For a dog between the ages of six months to one year, two meals are enough, and after the age of one a dog should have just one meal a day. A mixture of good-quality canned chicken or beef dog food, mixed with dry meal or bite-sized dog food, and some pet vitamins usually makes a good general diet. You can also get fresh meat instead of canned food and mix it with dry kibble or meal.

If your puppy is under ten weeks old, give it evaporated milk mixed with an equal amount of water to make about a quarter cup, and feed this to it in the morning and at night in addition to its solid food. This is for a medium-size puppy. Increase the amount for larger breeds and give a little less for toy breeds.

When you discontinue the noon and bedtime meals for an older puppy, you must increase the amount of food you give it for the remaining meals. A puppy should get approximately one ounce of food for each pound of body weight. Full-grown dogs should only get about half an ounce per pound of body weight.

Don't feed your puppy at the table. A small puppy that begs for a tidbit is very cute, but a grown dog that bothers everyone at mealtime is a nuisance. Not all the foods that people eat are good for dogs. Don't feed candy and other sweets to your pet, and never give it poultry bones or fish bones. Fresh water should always be available.

A young puppy has to relieve itself after every meal and after awaking from a nap. From the very first day, show your puppy where it may go and where it may not. Since a young puppy cannot control its bladder very well, many people find that it's more convenient to train their dogs to go in a certain spot lined with newspaper. This way, city people or working people do not have to take their pets outside so often.

If it uses the paper, praise it and make a fuss over it; if it does not, tell it firmly, "No!" and put it on the paper. You can get a special preparation in pet stores to encourage a puppy to relieve itself on the treated area; or you can put a little previously soiled paper on the spot. It won't take the puppy long to get the idea. If you train it to go outdoors from the start, be sure you let it out before an accident happens indoors. Praise it lavishly if it does the right thing.

Even after a puppy has learned where to relieve itself, accidents will happen. When you come into a room and see your

puppy looking guilty and unhappy, you can be sure to find a puddle in a corner. Or, when you take your puppy outdoors, it will sniff, play hide-and-seek, chew on sticks and other objects it finds, or run to greet the neighbor's dog instead of doing what it was supposed to do. As soon as you bring it back into the house, it will make its puddle. Be patient and firm. Tell it "No!" and take it outdoors again.

The time will come very soon—usually in about two weeks—when your puppy will let you know when it wants to go out by sitting, jumping, or barking at the door. The older the puppy gets, the longer it can control itself.

Teach your puppy or older dog good street manners right away. Curb your dog. If you walk your dog in public streets, in public parks, or in the suburbs, bring along some disposable plastic bags in which to put the droppings till you can throw them out, or use one of the scoopers specially designed for this purpose and available in pet stores. Most cities have laws requiring pet owners to keep their dogs on the leash and to clean up after them.

If you already have a dog, the new puppy will learn many things more quickly by following the example of the older dog. It will imitate the good and the bad habits of your other dog. Most grown dogs make friends easily with a puppy, but might resent an older dog. If you have a very possessive dog and think that it might resent the new puppy, try introducing them to each other outside your own home. Before bringing it home, take the new dog to a neighbor's or a friend's and then bring the older dog there. Don't do it the other way around. If you come in with a new puppy, the older dog will be jealous right away. Let them sniff each other and look each other over for a few minutes. Then you can take them both home together. Usually the older dog will be extremely patient and tolerant with a lively puppy, and will clean it, play with it, and guard it like a parent.

Your puppy will grow up quickly and almost daily you'll see changes in its looks and behavior. Dogs that have erect or semi-erect ears as adults (prick ears) usually have droopy ears in puppyhood. Then, when the puppy grows, one ear might stand up, the other hang down. A few days later the reverse might happen, and then both ears might hang down again.

Some breeds get their ears cropped and some get their tails docked, or both. This should be done early in a puppy's life; the breeder will tell you at what age to do it for your breed of dog. It is not necessary to conform to this fashion, and in England it has been outlawed. But if you intend to show your dog, you must abide by AKC rules and standards.

GREAT DANE

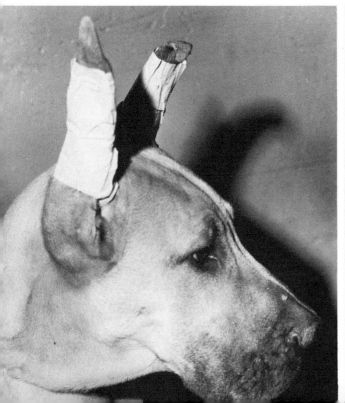

Just like small children, puppies go through various stages of behavior and get into all kinds of mischief. A normal puppy chews on things, gets into cupboards or closets, and upsets everything in them. It will pull out objects, collect and hide various kinds of clothing or household articles, get into everyone's way, and even nip sometimes. Most of the chewing a puppy does is to help its new teeth break through the gums. Give the puppy toys of its own or a marrow bone that it can chew on but not chew up. The bone can be boiled first or given with the marrow still in it. Don't give the puppy an old shoe or sock and then scold it if it chews up your new ones. The animal cannot distinguish between old and new articles. A puppy's toys should not be human clothing or household objects. Just as in housebreaking, use lavish praise or a firm "No" to let your dog know how you feel about what it has been doing.

If a puppy has to be left alone in the house for long periods, it becomes bored and will look for things to do that it would never do when someone is in the house with it. There is also a danger that it might hurt itself, get stuck somewhere, or get into a fight with another household pet. It also might get into

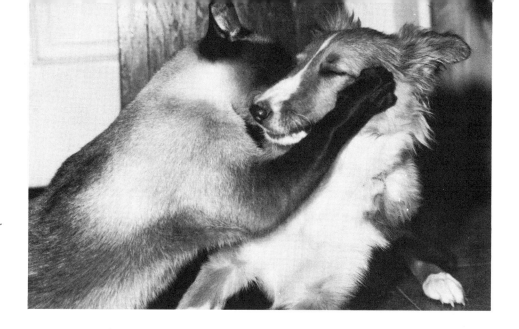

the habit of lolling about on the furniture. The more intelligent the puppy is, the more various the mischief it can think up. Get a friend or neighbor to look in on your small puppy, and feed it, take it outside, and play with it for a few minutes. But teach the puppy soon that you will return. Many dogs bark incessantly when their owners are away, and this can cause much bad feeling between neighbors. Teach the puppy to remain quiet when alone. Start out by leaving it for just a few minutes, listening behind the door or nearby. If the puppy is quiet, return and praise it and even give it a tidbit. If it barks or howls, rush back in and show it that you are angry. Tell it harshly "No!" or "Quiet!" You may even slap a rolled-up newspaper loudly on a table or against the wall to startle the dog. Repeat it a few times, and the puppy will get the idea. It will learn to await your return in a confident and relaxed way.

When you return to your puppy after a period of absence, be sure you give it your undivided attention and a happy playtime. Play, romp, or walk with your puppy. Do not let it bother the neighbors, or chase after cars or other dogs. Leash laws are in effect in most communities. Observe them, or your puppy might get into trouble or even get killed on the road.

A brief daily grooming period should be something your puppy enjoys. Place it on a table or bench (if it is a small dog) on which you have spread newspapers or an old towel so that the puppy does not slip. Brush it with a stiff brush first, and then comb gently. Short-haired dogs need only brushing. Long-haired dogs need to have tangles combed out. Do not pull the hair; work on a small area at a time; and talk soothingly to your

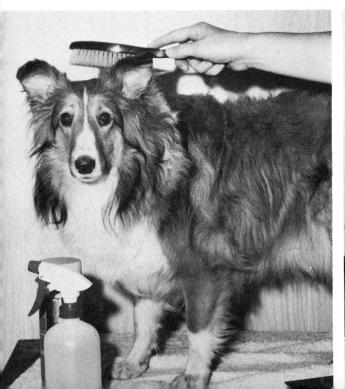
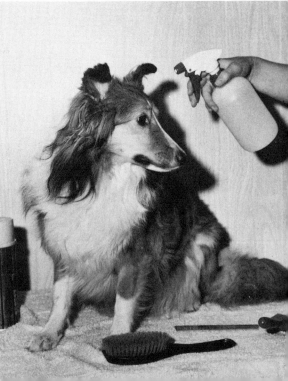

dog while you groom it. Bathe your puppy only when very necessary. If it is just a little dirty, use a dry shampoo or foam that is sprayed on and rubbed in. Follow the directions and brush out thoroughly. Ears can be cleaned with a cotton swab dipped into rubbing alcohol, but don't go deep into the sensitive ear.

A dog's toenails must be cut regularly if it does not wear them down on rough outdoor surfaces. Special clippers must be used for this, and your veterinarian can show you how to use them so you will not cut too deep.

There are many dog-grooming parlors for breeds that need professional attention. Some dogs are plucked, some are clipped or stripped. Some breeds need to have only light clipping or scissoring to give them a neat appearance. Others, like little

MINIATURE POODLE   YORKSHIRE TERRIER

Yorkshire Terriers that are groomed for the show ring, get their long, silky hair oiled and wrapped in tiny waxed tissue-paper packages to prevent soiling or breaking. The hair is brushed out just before they enter the show ring. Many strange styles have been invented for clipping poodles. These are not necessary to the well-being of the dog, but are only to please the owner's sense of fashion.

If you do not want to spend money on professional grooming and do not have much time to groom the animal yourself, get a short-haired breed of puppy.

Every puppy should learn to obey, regardless of whether it is to be a city or a country pet, a hunting dog or a lap and house dog, or a contestant in a show or obedience trial.

Since the beginning of its friendship with man, the dog has been known for its eagerness to please. It will work for praise alone. Never beat your dog and break its spirit. It is a sorry sight to see a dog cower and cringe when called, always afraid of punishment. If your dog comes to you when you call it, wagging its tail, looking trustingly and attentively at you, you know you have done your job well. The right kind of discipline is a special kind of love, and is reflected in your dog's proud behavior.

The best way to train your dog is to join an obedience class. Such classes are held almost everywhere—check with your local dog club, 4-H Club, Y.M.C.A., or animal welfare organization. Any of these places may conduct obedience classes or can tell you where they are held. Some public schools have also re-

SHETLAND SHEEPDOG, ENGLISH SPRINGER SPANIEL, IRISH SETTER,
KEESHOND, SHETLAND SHEEPDOG

cently started obedience training programs. Some of these courses are free, others require a nominal fee. They are great fun for both you and your dog.

Training can start when your puppy is only four months old. But do not expect too much of it at that age, and keep the sessions very short. Five or ten minutes once or twice a day is enough.

Teaching the puppy to come when called is usually the best beginning. Put a light lead on its collar (a six-foot nylon one is used by professionals), or get a slip-on lead with an adjustable clip. Call the puppy to you and praise it if it comes. If it does not come, pull it gently but firmly to you. Use its name and the word "Come" when you call. Always use the same word. Praise it or reward it when it reaches you, even if you had to pull it toward you.

Between the ages of six months and one year the dog can be taught in earnest. The saying "You can't teach an old dog new tricks" is not correct. Most dogs will learn even if they are quite old, though puppies do learn much more rapidly. Many books explain basic training in detail, but training in a competitive group is much better for the dog. The basic commands every dog should learn are:

Heel: Walking with you on your left side, while you hold the leash loosely in front of you in your right hand. When you stop, your dog should stop also and sit down on your left.

Stay: Staying where you tell it to, even if you walk out of sight for a few minutes.

Sit: Sitting down.

Down: Lying down.

Come: Coming to you and sitting down in front of you, till you give the command *Heel*. Then the dog should return to your left side and sit down again.

HEEL

HEEL AND HALT

SIT AND STAY

DOWN AND STAY

COME AND HEEL

A well-mannered dog is a joy to live with, the pride of its owner, admired by friends, and perhaps even a prize-winner in the obedience ring.

The little soft ball of fur will soon be grown up. Make the most of its happy puppyhood. The work and the worries will all have been worthwhile when your pet grows into a trusted, loyal, healthy family member, in whose eyes you can do no wrong, and who will share your life for many years.

INDEX

References to photographs are printed in boldface type.

Abandoned puppy, giving a home to, 14
Afgan Hound, **10**
Age considerations, 16–18
  for discipline training, 43, 44
  when feeding, 29–30
Air freight, shipping by, 23
Alone, leaving (for long periods), 38–39
  barking and, 39
  giving attention to (when returning), 40
Altering (operation), 20
American Kennel Club (AKC), 6, 13, 22, 36
Animal shelters, buying from, 14
Arrival of new puppy, planning in advance for, 21

Baby panties, 20
Barking or howling, 39
Bathing and brushing, 41
Beagle, **8, 9**
Beef dog food, 30
Bichon Frise, **9**

Box:
  for carrying, 23
  for sleeping, 26
  for taking home, 23–24
Breeds:
  kinds of, 6–8
  number of, 6
  oriented to one master, 17
Bulldog, **7**

Canned dog food, 30
Car-sickness, 25
Certificate of registration, 22
Chewing, 30, 37
Chicken dog food, 30
Christmas, puppies at, 21
Cocker Spaniel, **8, 13**
Collar, checking for re-adjustment of, 26
Collie, 17
Come (command), 43, 44
Crying and yapping, 28
Curbing your dog, 33

Dalmation, **8**
Dealers, buying from, 13–14

Discipline training, 42–47
  age to start, 43, 44
  basic commands, 44
  classes, 42–43
  in a competitive group, 44
  lead collar for, 43
Doberman, 17
Dog shows, 8
Doggie britches, 20
Down (command), 44
Droopy ears, 36
Droppings, scooping up, 33
Dry food, 30

Ears:
  cleaning, 41
  cropping, 36
English Springer Spaniel, **7, 8, 43**
Evaporated milk, 30

Father (sire), 13
Females, 18–20
  in "heat," 20
  spayed, 20

Food and feeding, 29–30
   amount of, 30
   at the table, 30
4-H Club, 42
Fox Terrier, Toy, **7**
Furniture, lolling about
   on, 39

German Shepherd, **10,**
   17, 28, **34–35**
Great Dane, **36**
Great Pyrenees, 6, **10**
Grooming, 40–42
   bathing and brushing,
   40–41
   parlors for, 41
   for the show ring, 42
   toenails, 41
Guard duty, 18

Health certificate, 18
Heel (command), 44
Hot-water bag, 28
Humane Society, buying
   from, 14

Inoculations, 18
Irish Setter, **43**
Irish Wolfhound, 6

Keeshound, **43**
Kennels, 21, 22
   buying from, 13–14
   reputation of, 13

Lead collar, 43
Leash laws, 33, 40
Lhasa Apso, **8**
Litters, of mongrels, 16
Long-hairs, brushing, 40

Males, 18–20
   aggressiveness of, 18
   altered, 20
   fur of, 20
   size of, 18
Mastiff, 17
Mischief, 38–39
Mongrels, 14–16, **15**
Mother (dam), 13

Name, calling by, 26

Obedience classes, 42–43
Obedience work, 18
Older dog, new puppy
   with, 34

Papers, *see* Certificate of
   registration
Paws, telling size of dog
   by, 14
Pedigree certificate, 22
Pet stores, 21, 33
   buying from, 13–14
Picking up and handling,
   26
   to put in a box, 23–24
Poodles, **8, 32, 41**
   clipping of, 42
Prick ears, 36
Pug, **10**
Punishment, what not to
   do, 42

Registration, 6, 13
   dam and sire, 13
   papers, 22

St. Bernard, 6, **7, 10,** 28
Seeing-eye dog, 18

Shampoo, 41
Shetland Sheepdog
   (Sheltie), **2, 5, 16–
   40, 43, 44–47**
Shih Tzu, **8**
Short-hairs, brushing, 40
Show dogs, 13
   grooming, 42
Sit (command), 44
Sleeping quarters, 26
   in your bed, 28
Spaying (operation), 20
Stay (command), 44
Sticks, chewing on, 30
Street manners, 33

Tails, docked, 36
Temperament and size, 9
Toenails, cutting, 41
Toilet training, 30–33
   accidents, 31–33
   with newspapers, 31
   street manners, 33
   telling "No!," 33
Toys, 37

Veterinarian check-up,
   14, 18, 20
Vitamins, 30

Water, fresh, 30
Welsh Terrier, **11,** 12, **12**
West Highland White
   Terrier, **8**
Worming, 18

Y.M.C.A., 42
Yorkshire Terrier, **10,
   11,** 11–12, **12, 41,** 42

7